Keep your weight in check after your bariatric surgery

Useful tips and tricks for cooking

Emily Sparker

Table of Contents

Cabbage Diet Soup

Prep Time:

Active Time: 35 mins Total Time: 55 mins Servings: 6

Ingredient:

- tablespoons extra-virgin olive oil 1 medium onion, chopped
- 2 medium carrots, chopped 2 stalks celery, chopped
- 1 medium red bell pepper, chopped 2 cloves garlic, minced
- 1 ½ teaspoon Italian seasoning
- ½ teaspoon ground pepper
- ¼ teaspoon salt
- 8 cups low-sodium vegetable broth
- medium head green cabbage, halved and sliced 1 large tomato, chopped
- teaspoons white-wine vinegar

Instructions:

- Heat oil in a large pot over medium heat. Add onion, carrots, and celery. Cook, stirring until the vegetables begin to soften, 6 to 8 minutes. Add bell pepper, garlic, Italian seasoning, pepper, and salt and cook, stirring, for 2 minutes.

- Add broth, cabbage, and tomato; increase the heat to medium-high and bring to a boil. Reduce heat to maintain a simmer, partially cover, and cook until all the vegetables are tender, 15 to 20 minutes more. Remove from heat and stir in vinegar.

Nutrient Value:

Calories: 133| Protein: 3g| Carbohydrates: 19.8g| Dietary Fiber: 7g| Sugars: 11g| Fat: 5.2g| Saturated Fat: 0.7g| Vitamin C: 88.2mg| Calcium: 110.7mg| Iron: 1.5mg| Magnesium: 30.2mg| Potassium: 504.1mg|Sodium: 451.1m

Veg Cutlet Recipe (Air Fryer Recipe + No Breadcrumbs)

Prep Time:

15 Mins Cook Time: 40 Mins Total Time: 55 Mins

Ingredients: For Cutlets:

- cups Sweet Potatoes (Boiled, Peeled and Mashed) 1 cup is 250 ml 3/4 cup Carrot (finely grated)
- 1/2 cup Sweet Corn (steamed)
- 1/2 cup Capsicum (finely chopped) 1/3 cup Green Peas (Steamed)
- 1/2 cup Quick Cooking Oats Or Instant Oats 1 tbsp Ginger Paste
- & 1/2 tbsp Oil For Cooking cutlets (1 tbsp oil is 15 ml) Salt to taste
- to 3 tbsp Coriander Leaves (finely chopped) Spices
- tsp Kashmiri Red chili powder 1 tsp is 5 ml 1 & 1/2 tsp Garam Masala Powder
- 1/2 tsp Turmeric Powder
- 1/4 tsp Chaat Masala Powder
- 1/2 tsp Amchur Powder or Dry Mango Powder

Instructions:

- In a wide bowl, add boiled and mashed sweet potatoes, cooked peas, steamed sweet corn, grated carrots, and finely chopped capsicum.

- Add all the spices, ginger paste, quick-cooking oats, and salt to taste. Now add the finely chopped coriander leaves (I have used stems as well).

- Mix everything together.

- Divide and take an equal portion of the cutlet mixture and shape them into an "oval" shape. Once the cutlets are shaped, preheat the Air Fryer at 200 Degrees C for 5 minutes

- Place around 12 cutlets, brush or spray oil and cook them for 15 minutes at 200 Degree C.

- Turn them after 8 to 10 minutes of cooking, repeat the process of spraying oil or brushing and air fry them until they are golden brown.

- Serve with the accompaniment of your choice.

Nutrient Value:

Calories: 572kcal | Carbohydrates: 1g | Protein: 46g | Fat: 43g | Saturated Fat: 22g | Cholesterol: 168mg | Sodium: 219mg | Potassium: 606mg | Sugar: 1g | Calcium: 16mg | Iron: 4mg

Air-Fried Crispy Vegetables

Prep Time:

10 Mins Cook Time: 15 Mins

Ingredients:

- Cups mixed vegetables(bell peppers, cauliflower, mushrooms, zucchini, baby corn) For batter
- 1/4 cup cornstarch(cornflour in india) 1/4 cup all-purpose flour/maida
- ½ tsp garlic powder
- ½-1 tsp red chilli powder
- ½-1 tsp black pepper powder 1 tsp salt or as per taste
- tsp oil
- For Sauce Mix
- tbsp soy sauce
- 1 tbsp chilli sauce/
- 1 tbsp tomato ketchup
- 1 tbsp vinegar(rice/synthetic or apple cider) 1 tsp brown sugar/coconut sugar
- Other
- 1 tbsp sesame oil or any plant-based oil 1 tsp sesame seeds
- Spring onion greens for garnish

Instructions:

- Cut Cauliflower in small florets, cubed bell peppers, cut mushrooms in half, and carrots and zucchini in circles. Do not cut very thin strips.

- Make a batter with all-purpose flour, cornstarch(sold as cornflour in India), garlic powder, bell pepper powder, red chili powder, and salt.

- Add a tsp of oil and make a smooth lump-free batter. Add and coat all the vegetables nicely in the batter.

- Preheat the air fryer at 350F, then add the veggies when indicated. Air fry the veggies, it takes about 10 minutes.

- Make the sauce mix. In a heavy-bottomed pan, heat a tbsp of oil, add finely chopped garlic, sauté till it gives aroma, and then add the sauce mix and freshly ground black pepper.

- Cook for a minute then add the air fried vegetables and mix well with light hands. Coat all the veggies nicely in sauce.

- Sprinkle Sesame Seeds and finely chopped spring onion greens and serve hot.

For Sauce Mix.

- Mix all the **Ingredients:** together listed under the Saucesection. For the deep-fried version.

- Coat vegetables in batter nicely and then deep fry in hot oil, till light brown in color. Oil should be hot enough so that the veggies remain crispy. Take out and cool down and then add to the sauce mix.

Nutrient Value:

Total fat: 3.7g sodium: 1820.8mg sugar: 11.3g Vitamin A: 169.2ug

Carbohydrates: 33.6mg Protein:18g

Vitamin C: 165.5mg

Air Fryer Roasted Brussels Sprouts

Prep Time:

5 Minutes Cook Time: 18 Minutes Total Time: 23 Minutes

Ingredients:

- 1 pound Brussels sprouts 1 ½ tablespoon olive oil
- ½ teaspoon salt
- ½ teaspoon black pepper

Instructions:

- Preheat the air fryer to 390 degrees. Wash Brussels sprouts and pat dry. Remove any loose leaves.

- If the sprouts are larger cut them in half. Place Brussels sprouts into a bowl.

- Drizzle olive oil over the vegetables.

- Stir to make sure the Brussels sprouts are fully coated. Place the Brussels sprouts in the basket.

- Season with salt and pepper.

- Cook for 15 to 18 minutes or until the Brussels sprouts soften and begin to brown.

- Serve immediately.

Nutrient Value:

Calories: 172 Total Fat: 11g Saturated Fat: 2g

Unsaturated Fat: 9g

Sodium: 577mg Carbohydrates: 16g Fiber: 6g

Sugar: 4g Protein: 6g

Air Fryer Roasted Broccoli (Low Carb + Keto)

Prep Time:

Yield: 4 Cook Time: 8 Minutes Total Time: 8 Minutes

Ingredients:

- 5 cups broccoli florets 2 tablespoons butter
- 2 teaspoons minced garlic
- 1/3 cup shredded parmesan cheese Salt and pepper to taste
- Lemon slices (optional)

Instructions:

- Melt the butter and combine with the minced garlic, set aside for later. Preheat your air fryer according to the manufactures directions at a temperature of 350 degrees.

- Add the chopped broccoli florets to the basket of the air fryer and spray very lightly with cooking oil.

- Roast the broccoli for 8 minutes total. I remove the basket after 4 minutes and shake or toss with tongs to make sure everything is cooking evenly, then cook for 4 more minutes.

- At this point, the broccoli should be fork tender at the thickest part of the stem and slightly crispy on the outside.

- Remove the broccoli from the basket and toss with the garlic butter, parmesan and add salt and pepper to taste.

Nutrient Value:

Calories: 106| Total Fat: 7.9g| carbohydrates: 5.2g| fiber: 2.1g| protein: 5.3g

Mexican Cabbage Soup

Prep Time:

Total Time: 20 mins Servings: 8

Ingredient:

- 2 tablespoons extra-virgin olive oil 2 cups chopped onions
- 1 cup chopped carrot 1 cup chopped celery
- 1 cup chopped poblano or green bell pepper 4 large cloves garlic, minced
- 8 cups sliced cabbage
- 1 tablespoon tomato paste
- 1 tablespoon minced chipotle chiles in adobo sauce 1 teaspoon ground cumin
- ½ teaspoon ground coriander
- 4 cups low-sodium vegetable broth or chicken broth 4 cups water
- 2 (15 ounces) cans of low-sodium pinto or black beans, rinsed
- ¾ teaspoon salt
- ½ cup chopped fresh cilantro, plus more for serving 2 tablespoons lime juice

Instructions:

- Heat oil in a large soup pot (8-quart or larger) over medium heat. Add onions, carrot, celery, poblano (or bell pepper), and garlic; cook,stirring frequently, until softened, 10 to 12 minutes. Add cabbage; cook, stirring occasionally until slightly softened, about 10 minutes more. Add tomato paste, chipotle, cumin, and coriander; cook, stirring, for 1 minute more. Add broth, water, beans, and salt. Cover and bring to a boil over high heat. Reduce heat and simmer, partially covered, until the vegetables are tender about 10 minutes. Remove from heat and stir in cilantro and lime juice. Serve garnished with cheese, yogurt, and/or avocado, if desired.

Nutrient Value:

Calories: 167; Protein: 6.5g| Carbohydrates: 27.1g| Dietary Fiber: 8.7g| Sugars: 6.6g| Fat: 3.8g| Saturated Fat: 0.6g| Vitamin A: 2968.9IU|

Vitamin C: 47.2mg| Folate: 48.4mcg| Calcium: 115mg| Iron: 2.3mg| Magnesium: 50.5mg| Potassium: 623.7mg| Sodium: 408.1mg|

Everything Bagel Avocado Toast

Prep Time:

Active Time: 5 mins Total Time: 5 mins Servings: 1

Ingredient:

- ¼ medium avocado, mashed
- slice whole-grain bread, toasted
- teaspoons everything bagel seasoning Pinch of flaky sea salt (such as Maldon)

Instructions:

- Spread avocado on toast. Top with seasoning and salt.

Nutrient Value:

Calories: 172; Protein: 5.4g| Carbohydrates: 17.8g| Dietary Fiber: 5.9g| Sugars: 2.3g| Fat: 9.8g| Saturated Fat: 1.4g| Vitamin C: 5.5mg| Calcium: 60.5mg| Iron: 1.3mg| Magnesium: 41.4mg| Potassium: 341.5mg| Sodium: 251.8mg| Added Sugar: 1g.

Quick Vegetable Saute

Prep Time:

Total Time: 15 mins Servings: 4

Ingredient:

- 1 tablespoon extra-virgin olive oil 1 small shallot, minced
- 4 cups mixed frozen vegetables, such as corn, carrots, and green beans
- ½ teaspoon dried dill or tarragon
- ¼ teaspoon salt
- ¼ teaspoon freshly ground pepper

Instructions:

- Heat oil in a large skillet over medium heat. Add shallot and cook, stirring, until softened, about 1 minute. Stir in frozen vegetables. Cover and cook, stirring occasionally, until the vegetables are tender, 4 to 6 minutes. Stir in dill (or tarragon), salt, and pepper.

Nutrient Value:

Calories: 107; Protein: 2.6g| Carbohydrates: 16.8g| Dietary Fiber: 3.5g|Sugars: 4.2g| Fat: 4.2g| Saturated Fat: 0.6g| Vitamin A: 6423.6IU| Vitamin C: 9.6mg| Folate: 28.3mcg| Calcium: 38.8mg| Iron: 0.9mg| Magnesium: 24mg| Potassium: 293.9mg| Sodium: 177.7mg| Thiamin: 0.1mg.

Air Fryer Frozen Vegetables (No More Mushy Frozen Broccoli!)

Prep Time:

5 Mins Cook Time: 20 Mins Total Time: 25 Mins

Ingredients: For Air Fryer Frozen Broccoli:

- 1 lb. frozen broccoli (do not thaw) 3 tablespoons avocado oil
- 1 teaspoon Trader Joe's Everything But the Bagel Seasoning (other seasoning blends may be substituted)
- cooking oil spray of choice
- Ingredients For Air Fryer Frozen Cauliflower:
- 1 lb. frozen cauliflower (do not thaw) 3 tablespoons avocado oil
- 1 teaspoon Trader Joe's Everything But the Bagel Seasoning (other seasoning blends may be substituted)
- cooking oil spray of choice

Ingredients: For Air Fryer Frozen Brussels Sprouts:

- 12 ounces frozen brussels sprouts (do not thaw) 2 tablespoons avocado oil
- 1 teaspoon trader joe's everything but the bagel seasoning (other
- seasoning blends may be substituted) Cooking oil spray of choice
- Ingredients For Air Fryer Frozen Spinach:
- 1 lb. Frozen whole leaf spinach (do not thaw) 3 tablespoons avocado oil
- 1 teaspoon trader joe's everything but the bagel seasoning (other seasoning blends may be substituted)
- Cooking oil spray of choice
- Ingredients For Air Fryer Frozen Okra:
- 12 ounces frozen okra, chopped (do not thaw) 2 tablespoons avocado oil

- 1 teaspoon Trader Joe's Everything But the Bagel Seasoning (other seasoning blends may be substituted)

- cooking oil spray of choice

- Ingredients For Air Fryer Frozen Butternut Squash:

- 10 ounces frozen butternut squash, chopped small (do not thaw) 2 tablespoons avocado oil

- 1 teaspoon trader joe's everything but the bagel seasoning (other seasoning blends may be substituted)

- Cooking oil spray of choice

Instructions:

How To Make Air Fryer Frozen Broccoli:

- Cut the frozen broccoli into smaller pieces if some of the pieces are large. (I did not need to do this.) Lightly mist your air fryer baking racks with the cooking spray.

- Drizzle the frozen broccoli with the oil and sprinkle with the seasoning. Stir to distribute it well.

- Spread the broccoli in a single layer on the racks. I used both racks that came with the oven. You may need to cook the broccoli in batches if you have a small air fryer.

- Make sure the drip tray is in place in your air fryer oven. Put the racks in the oven and roast at 400°F for 12 minutes.

- Switch the position of the trays in the oven. Bake an additional 8 minutes. That's it!

- How To Make Air Fryer Frozen Cauliflower:

- Cut the frozen cauliflower into smaller pieces if some of the pieces are large. (I did not need to do this.) Lightly mist your air fryer baking racks with the cooking spray.

- Drizzle the frozen cauliflower with the oil and sprinkle with the seasoning. Stir to distribute it well.

- Spread the cauliflower in a single layer on the racks. I used both racks that came with the oven. You may need to cook the cauliflower in batches if you have a small air fryer.

- Make sure the drip tray is in place in your air fryer oven. Put the racks in the oven and roast at 400°F for 12 minutes.

- Switch the position of the trays in the oven. Bake an additional 8 minutes.

How To Make Air Fryer Frozen Brussels Sprouts:

- Lightly mist your air fryer baking racks with the cooking spray.

- Drizzle the frozen Brussels sprouts with the oil and sprinkle with the seasoning. Stir to distribute it well.

- Spread the Brussels sprouts in a single layer on the racks. I used both racks that came with the oven. You may need to cook the Brussels sprouts in batches if you have a small air fryer.

- Make sure the drip tray is in place in your air fryer oven. Put the racks in the oven and roast at 400°F for 10 minutes.

- Switch the position of the trays in the oven. Bake an additional 8 minutes.

How To Make Air Fryer Frozen Spinach:

- Lightly mist your air fryer baking racks with the cooking spray.

- Drizzle the frozen spinach with the oil and sprinkle with the seasoning. Stir to distribute it well.

- Spread the spinach on the air fryer racks. I used both racks that came with the oven. Leave the spinach in frozen clumps for results that are both tender and crispy. Break up the frozen clumps for a spinach side dish that is more crispy.

- Make sure the drip tray is in place in your air fryer oven. Put the racks in the oven and roast at 400°F for 10 minutes.

- Flip and stir the spinach pieces. Switch the position of the trays in the oven. Bake an additional 10 minutes.

How To Make Air Fryer Frozen Okra:

- Lightly mist your air fryer baking racks with the cooking spray.

- Drizzle the frozen okra with the oil and sprinkle with the seasoning. Stir to distribute it well.

- Spread the okra in a single layer on the racks. I used both racks that came with the oven. You may need to cook the okra in batches if you have a small air fryer.

- Make sure the drip tray is in place in your air fryer oven. Put the racks in the oven and roast at 400°F for 12 minutes.

- Switch the position of the trays in the oven. Bake an additional 8 minutes.

How To Make Air Fryer Frozen Butternut Squash:

- Lightly mist your air fryer baking racks with the cooking spray.

- Drizzle the frozen winter squash with the oil and sprinkle with the seasoning. Stir to distribute it well.

- Spread the butternut squash in a single layer on the air fryer racks. I was able to fit it all on a single rack.

- Make sure the drip tray is in place in your air fryer oven. Put the rack in the top rack position in the oven and roast at 400°F for 20 minutes, stirring and flipping the squash after 12 minutes.

Nutrient Value:

Calories: 128kcal| Carbohydrates: 4g| Protein: 2g| Fat: 10.5g| Saturated Fat: 1.2g| Sodium: 100mg| Potassium: 180mg| Fiber: 2g

Roasted Vegetable Pasta Salad

Prep Time:

40 minutes

Cook Time: 1 hour 45 minutes

Total Time: 2 hours 25 minutes

Ingredients:

- eggplant (small)

- 1 tablespoon olive oil

- zucchini (medium-sized. Aka courgette. 1 tablespoon olive oil

- tomatoes (medium. Cut in eighths) 300 g pasta (large, shaped pasta. 4 cups) 2 bell peppers (any color)

- 175 g cherry tomatoes (sliced. Or tomatoes cut into small chunks. 1 cup)

- 2 teaspoons salt (or salt sub)

- 8 tablespoons parmesan cheese (grated)

- 125 ml italian dressing (bottled, fat free/ 1/2 cup / 4 oz) Basil (few leaves of fresh)

Instructions:

- Wash eggplant, slice off and discard the green end. Do not peel. Slice the eggplant into 1 cm (1/2 inch) thick rounds. If using a paddle-type air fryer such as an Actifry™, put in a pan with 1 tablespoon of olive oil. If using a basket-type such as an AirFryer™, toss with 1 tablespoon of olive oil and put in the basket. Cook for about 40 minutes until quite soft and no raw taste left. Set aside.

- Wash zucchini/courgette, slice off and discard the green end. Do not peel. Slice into 1 cm (1/2 inch) thick rounds. If using a paddle-type air fryer such as an Actifry™, put in a pan with 1 tablespoon of olive oil. If using a basket-type such as an AirFryer™, toss with 1 tablespoon of olive oil and put in the basket. Cook for about 25 minutes until quite soft and no raw taste left. Set aside.

- Wash and chunk the tomatoes. If using an Actifry 2 in 1, arranged in a top grill pan. If using a basket-type air fryer, arrange it in the basket. Spray lightly with cooking spray. Roast for about 30 minutes until reduced in size and starting to brown. Set aside.

- Cook the pasta according to pasta directions, empty into a colander, run cold water over it to wash some starch off, drain, set aside to cool.

- Wash, seed, and chop the bell pepper; put into a large bowl. Wash and slice the cherry tomatoes (or small-chunk the regular tomato); add to that bowl. Add the roast veggies, the pasta, the salt, the dressing, the chopped basil, and the parm, and toss all with your (clean) hands to mix well.

- Set in fridge to chill and marinate. Serve chilled or room temperature.

Nutrient Value:

Serving: 1g | Calories: 121kcal | Carbohydrates: 23g | Protein: 5g | Fat: 4g | Saturated Fat: 1g | Sodium: 417mg | Potassium: 471mg | Fiber: 4g | Sugar: 7g | Vitamin C: 34.2mg | Calcium: 53mg | Iron: 0.8mg

Air Fryer Buffalo Chicken Salad

Prep Time:

15 Mins Cook Time: 15 Mins Total Time: 30 Mins

Ingredients:

- 1 pound boneless, skinless chicken breasts, thick sides pounded to make an even thickness

- 1/2 cup WHOLE30 Buffalo Vinaigrette 6 cups chopped romaine lettuce

- 1 cup thinly sliced celery 1/2 cup shredded carrot

- 3-4 tbsp WHOLE30 Ranch Dressing

- small ripe avocado, peeled, pitted, and sliced 1 cup cherry tomatoes, halved

- Freshly ground black pepper 2 tsp finely chopped chives

Instructions:

- IN a large resealable plastic bag, combine chicken and WHOLE30 Buffalo Vinaigrette. Massage to coat. Seal bag and marinate in the refrigerator for at least 2 hours and up to 4 hours.

- PREHEAT air fryer* to 375°F. Remove chicken from bag; discard marinade. Add the chicken to the air fryer. Cook until chicken is no longer pink and the internal temperature is 170°F, turning once about 15 minutes. Let stand while making the salad.

- IN a large bowl, combine the romaine, celery, and carrot. Add the WHOLE30 Ranch Dressing; toss to combine. Divide salad among four serving plates.

- SLICE the chicken. Top the salads with sliced chicken, avocado, and cherry tomatoes. Season to taste with black pepper. Sprinkle with chives.

Nutrient Value:

Calories: 122| Fat: 8g| Sat fat: 2g| Unsatfat: 5g| Protein: 10g| Carbohydrate| 0g Fiber 0g| Sugars 0g| Added sugars: 0g| Sodium: 254mg

Cajun Potato Salad Recipe

Prep Time:

10 Minutes Cook Time: 20 Minutes Total Time: 30 Minutes

Ingredients:

- 1/2 lb red potatoes, quartered
- 2 tablespoons avocado oil (or grapeseed, coconut, or vegetable) 3 tablespoons The Fit Cook Southern Creole
- pinch of sea salt & pepper
- 2 slices cooked bacon, chopped and crumbled
- Salad Sauce
- 2/3 cup light mayo (I used olive oil mayo) 7oz 2% Greek yogurt
- 1/8 cup Dijon mustard (or more to taste) 5 BOILED eggs, chopped
- 1 cup diced Dill pickles (OR sweet if you prefer) 1/2 medium red onion, diced
- Sea salt & pepper to taste

Instructions:

- Set the air-fryer to 400F (or oven to 420F).

- In a large bowl, toss the sliced potatoes with oil and seasoning. Add the potatoes to the air-fryer basket. Air-fry for about 20 minutes, or until the potatoes are cooked through and the edges are crispy.

- Air-fried Cajun Potato Salad

- Mix the Ingredients for the sauce.

- Cook up some bacon in a skillet until crispy.

- Allow the pieces to cool on a paper towel, then chop into pieces.

- Once the potatoes have finished air-frying, LIGHTLY mash about 40-50% of the potatoes in a bowl, then fold in the remaining potatoes and mix. Add the sauce and the remaining Ingredients and fold everything together.

- Season to taste using salt & pepper, dill (or sweet) pickles, mustard, or Greek yogurt. Cover with plastic and store in the fridge for at least 20 minutes, but it's much better overnight.

Nutrient Value:

Calories: 491 Protein: 20g Fat: 16g Carbs: 72g Fiber: 5g Sugar: 9g

Air Fryer Squash With Kale Salad

Prep Time:

5 minutes Cook Time: 10 minutes Total Time: 15 minutes

Ingredients:

- Squash
- 1 medium delicata squash (see note 1) Salt and pepper to taste (or other spices) Salad
- 8 oz kale or other green, chopped
- 1 cup grape or cherry tomatoes, halved 2 cups cucumber, sliced
- 1/2 cup pomegranate seeds
- 1/4 cup squash seeds, roasted, optional 1/2 avocado, sliced, optional
- 1/2 cup vegan honey mustard dressing, or any dressing

Instructions:

- **Cut The Squash:** If using delicata, cut the top and bottom off, then slice it lengthwise down the middle. Cut the delicata (or other squash) into half-inch thick pieces. You can leave delicate in a half-ring shape, or you can slice it into smaller pieces (especially if feeding littles) (bigger is fine, but will take longer to cook). If you find the squash hard to cut, try microwaving it for a minute or two first.

- **Save The Seeds:** I highly recommend saving the seeds and roasting them! It's so easy, and worth it. I find it easiest to scoop out the seeds and membrane with a grapefruit spoon. Then fill a medium-sized bowl with water, so that the seeds mostly float to the top as I free them from the membrane.

- **Season:** Lightly spray the squash with water, (or oil, if that's your thing) and season with salt, pepper, and whatever else you like (sometimes I use garlic, chili, etc.)

- **Air Fryer Method:** Add to your air fryer. They will get crispier if they are in a single layer. Air fry at 375 degrees F (or 191 degrees C) for about 10 minutes, shaking halfway through. If you like it more browned, you can keep cooking for another 5 minutes or so.

- **Oven Method:** Line a baking tray with a silicone baking mat or parchment paper. Lay the squash pieces out in a single layer with a little breathing room (about an inch) between each piece. Bake at 400 degrees Fahrenheit (or 205 degrees Celsius) for about 20-25 minutes, flipping the pieces halfway through.

- **Store:** Refrigerate leftovers in an airtight container. The salad will keep for about 3 days (if dressed), the squash about 5 days (keep separate from the salad if possible). The seeds should keep on the counter in an airtight container for about 5 days.

Nutrient Value:

Calories: 213 Total Fat: 5.2g Sodium: 419.8mg Sugar: 23.6g

Carbohydrates: 37.1mg Protein:7.1g

Vitamin C: 165.5mg

Fried Chickpeas In The Air Fryer

Prep Time:

2 minutes Cook Time: 12 minutes Total Time: 14 minutes

Ingredients:

- 1/2 cups chickpeas 1 15 ounces can drain & rinse Spritz cooking spray
- teaspoons Nutrientsal yeast flakes 1/2 teaspoon granulated onion
- Pinch salt

Instructions:

- Put the drained chickpeas into the air fryer basket. Set the air fryer for 400 degrees and 12 minutes.

- Cook the plain chickpeas for the first 5 minutes. This will dry them out. Then open the basket, spritz the chickpeas with oil, give a shake, and spritz them again. Sprinkle on Nutrient Value **Facts**al yeast flakes, granulated onion, and a pinch of salt.

- Return the basket to the air fryer and cook for the remaining 7 minutes. Test a chickpea to see if it's done enough for you. Depending on your air fryer, the softness of your chickpeas, and your personal preferences, you may want to cook them for an additional 3 to 5 minutes. If desired, add another pinch of salt before serving.

Nutrient Value:

Calories: 105kcal | Carbohydrates: 17g | Protein: 5g | Fat: 1g | Sodium: 4mg | Potassium: 198mg | Fiber: 4g | Sugar: 2g | Vitamin A: 15IU | Vitamin C: 0.8mg | Calcium: 30mg | Iron: 1.8mg

Air Fryer Buffalo Chicken Tenders Salad

Prep Time:

15 minutes Cook Time: 25 minutes Total Time: 40 minutes

Ingredients:

- Chicken Tenders:
- ½ cup blanched almond flour 1 tsp sea salt
- tsp paprika
- ¼ tsp ground black pepper
- large chicken breasts, sliced lengthwise into ½" strips
- ¼ cup tapioca flour
- 2 tbsp garlic-infused olive oil Avocado oil cooking spray
- Salad:
- 2 hearts of romaine, chopped
- 1 cup carrots, coarsely-shredded 1 cup grape tomatoes, halved
- 1 bunch scallions, green tops only, chopped 1 red pepper, diced
- Your other favorite salad ingredients
- Ranch Dressing:
- ½ Batch of my dairy-free homemade ranch dressing recipe (paleo, whole30, low fodmap)
- Buffalo Sauce:
- ⅓ cup Paleo Low-FODMAP hot sauce 3 tbsp ghee, melted
- tbsp garlic-infused olive oil
- ½ tbsp coconut aminos

Instructions:

- Preheat the air fryer to 370° F for 10 minutes. While your air fryer preheats, combine almond flour, sea salt, paprika, and pepper in a large bowl, whisk to combine, and set aside. Place chicken strips in another

- large bowl. Add tapioca flour to the bowl and toss with your hands to coat the strips evenly. Add the garlic-infused oil and toss again to coat. Dredge each strip in the almond flour mixture, shaking off the excess, and set on a plate.

- Once your air fryer has preheated, spray the pan with cooking spray. Using tongs, place half of the breaded chicken strips in the pan in one layer, ideally not touching one another. Spray the strips lightly with cooking spray. Air fry for 12 minutes, flipping halfway through. Once the first batch has cooked, place it on a clean plate using a clean set of tongs and set aside. Using tongs, take one of the thickest strips out of the air fryer and check its temperature using an instant-read thermometer. The temperature of cooked chicken should be at least 165° F (75° C) to be safely consumed. Once the first batch is at the proper temperature, repeat these steps for the second half of the strips.

- While the chicken strips are frying, prepare a half-batch of my dairy-free homemade ranch dressing recipe, cover, and refrigerate until ready to serve. Chop the ingredients under "salad," place in a large serving bowl, and refrigerate.

- A minute or two before the chicken strips are done, in a large bowl, add the ingredients under "buffalo sauce," whisk to combine, and set aside until all the chicken strips are cooked. If the sauce solidifies, microwave it (covered) for about 20 seconds and whisk again.

- Once the second batch of strips has finished cooking, if desired, place the first batch back in the air fryer on top of the second batch and air fry at 370° F for a minute or so until heated (I typically skip this step as they're going on a cold salad anyway). Using tongs, take each strip out of the air fryer, dip in the buffalo sauce until fully-coated, and place it on a plate. Chop strips horizontally into small pieces if desired and serve on top of the salad with the ranch dressing.

Nutrient Value:

Total Fat: 30.8gg Sodium: 1321.9mg Sugar: 6.7g Vitamin A: 567.5ug

Carbohydrates: 21.4g Protein:29.8g

Vitamin C: 56.8mg

Roasted Salmon With Fennel Salad In An Air Fryer

Prep Time:

Active Time: 15 Mins Total Time: 25 Mins

Ingredients:

- teaspoons chopped fresh flat-leaf parsley 1 teaspoon finely chopped fresh thyme 1 teaspoon kosher salt, divided 4 (6-oz.) skinless center-cut salmon fillets 2 tablespoons olive oil 4 cups thinly sliced fennel (from 2 [15-oz.] heads fennel) 2/3 cup 2% reduced-fat Greek yogurt 1 garlic clove, grated 2 tablespoons fresh orange juice (from 1 orange) 1 teaspoon fresh lemon juice (from 1 lemon) 2 tablespoons chopped fresh dill

Instructions:

- Your air fryer has more up its sleeve than the expected crispy tricks— it's also a fantastic oven for roasting meaty fish fillets like salmon. This recipe serves four, but you can easily cut it in half to make a date night dinner for two.

- Everything comes together so easily—while the salmon cooks, whip up the quick and tangy fennel slaw. By the time you're finished, the salmon will be hot and ready to plate up. For a little extra heft, serve this meal with a side of your favorite quick-cooking brownrice.

- Try it with the air-fryer broccoli with cheese sauce, also pictured.

Nutrient Value:

Calories: 464| Fat: 30g |Sat fat: 7g| Unsatfat: 21g| Protein: 38g

|Carbohydrate: 9g| Fiber: 3g| Sugars: 5g| Added sugars: 0g |Sodium: 635mg

Air Fryer Healthy Southwestern Salad

Prep Time:

5 mins Cook Time: 8 mins Total Time: 13 mins

Ingredients:

- Kitchen Gadgets:
- Air Fryer
- Air Fryer Grill Pan Salad Bowl
- Southwestern Salad Recipe Ingredients
- 600 g Chickpeas
- Medium Red Pepper 200 g Frozen Sweetcorn 2 Celery Sticks
- ¼ Medium Cucumber
- ½ Small Red Onion
- Tbsp Extra Virgin Olive Oil 1 Tsp Grainy Mustard
- ¼ Tsp Garlic Powder 1 Tsp Basil
- 2 Tsp Mexican Seasoning Salt & Pepper

Instructions:

- Drain and rinse your chickpeas. Chop your red pepper into bite-size cubes. Load into the air fryer basket with the grill attachment the chickpeas, sweetcorn, and pepper. Sprinkle with Mexican seasoning and salt and pepper and cook for 8 minutes at 180c/360f.

- While the air fryer is in action, prep the rest of your salad. Peel and thinly slice your red onion. Clean and thinly dice your cucumber and celery. Load all three into a salad bowl.

- Mix extra virgin olive oil, basil, grainy mustard, and garlic powder. Pour into your salad bowl and mix.

- When the air fryer beeps, load in the ingredients and mix a little more. Serve or store into containers for later.

Nutrient Value:

Calories: 384kcal | Carbohydrates: 58g | Protein: 16g | Fat: 12g | Saturated Fat: 2g | Sodium: 44mg | Potassium: 737mg | Fiber: 15g | Sugar: 12g | | Vitamin C: 45mg | Calcium: 127mg | Iron: 6mg

Kale Salad with Air Fryer Herb Chicken Breast

Prep Time:

20 mins Cook Time: 20 mins Total Time: 40 mins

Ingredients:

- Tablespoon Panko (Bread Crumbs)
- Tablespoons Mixed Dry Herbs Use your favorite blend 1 Teaspoon Smoked Paprika
- 1 Teaspoon Salt
- 1 Tablespoon Olive Oil
- 1.5 Pounds Chicken Breast Pounded Evenly
- Cup Corn Kernels From about 2 years, if fresh 8 Strawberries, Sliced & Quartered
- 1/2 Ounce Goat Cheese
- Avocados, halved and sliced 2 Hard Boiled Eggs, sliced
- 2 Tablespoons Extra Virgin Olive Oil
- 16 Ounce Bag Baby Kale Greens (Washed & Ready)

Instructions:

- Combine panko, herbs, smoked paprika, salt, and olive oil in a small bowl to make a paste. Apply this evenly to the chicken breast.

- Cook the chicken in a preheated air fryer for 20 minutes at 370 degrees. Let it rest outside of the air fryer for 5 minutes before slicing for the salad

- In a large salad bowl or serving plate, place your bed of salad greens and then add the corn, strawberries, goat cheese, avocado, hard-boiled eggs, and chicken

- Drizzle the extra virgin olive oil over the top and then season lightly with salt and pepper

Nutrient Value:

Calories: 572kcal | Carbohydrates: 1g | Protein: 46g | Fat: 43g | Saturated Fat: 22g | Cholesterol: 168mg | Sodium: 219mg | Potassium: 606mg | Sugar: 1g | Calcium: 16mg | Iron:4mg

Easy Air Fryer Broccoli

Prep Time:

5 Minutes Cook Time: 6 Minutes Total Time: 11 Minutes

Ingredients:

- 2 heads of broccoli, cut into bite-sized pieces 2 tablespoons olive oil
- Sea salt, to taste
- Fresh cracked black pepper, to taste

Instructions:

- heads of broccoli, cut into bite-sized pieces 2 tablespoons olive oil
- Sea salt, to taste
- Fresh cracked black pepper, to taste

Nutrient Value:

Calories: 126| Total Fat: 8g| Saturated Fat: 1g| Trans Fat: 0g| Unsaturated Fat: 6g| Cholesterol: 0mg| Sodium: 222mg| Carbohydrates: 14g| Fiber: 6g| Sugar: 3g| Protein: 4g

Air Fryer Taco Salad Bowls

Prep Time:

1 Minute Cook Time: 7 Minutes Total Time: 8 Minutes

Ingredients:

- burrito sized flour tortilla Cooking spray

Instructions:

- Spray both sides of the tortilla with cooking spray.

- Fold a piece of foil double thickness the size of the tortilla. Fold into the basket of your air fryer.

- Place a larger ramekin (or something similar) into the middle of the shell.

- Air fry for 5 minutes at 400 degrees.

- Carefully remove ramekin (it's HOT!!) and foil. Place ramekin back into the center, air fry 2 minutes more.

Nutrient Value:

Calories: 220| Total Fat: 20g| Saturated Fat: 7g| Trans Fat: 0g| Unsaturated Fat: 11g| Cholesterol: 29mg| Sodium: 1321mg| Carbohydrates: 84g| Fiber: 11g| Sugar: 5g| Protein: 21g

Air Fryer, Grilled Chicken Caesar Salad

Prep Time:

5 Minutes Cook Time: 10 Minutes Additional Time: 5 Minutes Total Time: 20 Minutes

Ingredients:

- Grilled Chicken:

- boneless skinless chicken breast, about 5 ounces each 2 tablespoons chicken seasoning (i used lawry's)

- Olive oil spray

- Salad:

- 1/2 cup garlic croutons

- 1/4 cup caesar salad dressing

- 2 cups shredded romaine lettuce 1/3 cup shredded Parmesan cheese

Instructions:

- Rub the chicken seasoning all over the chicken

- As you coat them place them in either a greased air fryer basket or on a greased air fryer tray. Once you are all done coating your chicken, spray them with olive oil spray (the entire chicken breast, otherwise you will get white spots on your chicken)

- Set the temperature to 350 degrees F, for 5-10 minutes. (air fryer setting)

- When the time is up, make sure that the internal temperature reads at least: 165 degrees F.

- In a large mixing bowl, add the lettuce, shredded parmesan cheese, and salad dressing.

- Mix well.

- Cut up the chicken and add it on top. Plate, serve, and enjoy!

Nutrient Value:

Calories: 212| Total Fat: 7g| Saturated Fat: 2g| Unsaturated Fat: 0g| Cholesterol: 83mg| Sodium: 282mg| Carbohydrates: 2g| Fiber: 1g| Sugar: 1g| Protein: 33g

Air Fryer Brussel Sprout Caesar Salad

Prep Time:

2 mins COOK TIME: 15 mins

Ingredients:

- 10 oz Brussel sprouts, cut the ends off
- 4 tbsp Caesar dressing, storebought or homemade 2 tbsp shaved parmesan
- 1/4 cup garlic croutons

Instructions:

- Cut the ends off of the Brussel sprouts and with your hands flake them apart. The more loose pieces, the more crispy crunchy pieces!

- Add to the air fryer basket and drizzle with olive oil, season with salt and pepper.

- Air fry for 15 minutes at 375 until many of the edges and pieces are brown and crispy

- Transfer to a salad bowl, drizzle with caesar dressing, top with parmesan and croutons.

Nutrient Value:

Calories: 122| Fat: 8g| Sat fat: 2g| Unsatfat: 5g| Protein: 10g| Carbohydrate| 0g Fiber 0g| Sugars 0g| Added sugars: 0g| Sodium: 254mg

Crispy Chicken Cobb Salad

Prep Time:

15 mins Total Time: 15 mins

Ingredients:

- 3 oz of cooked chicken strips (I like Tyson) hard-boiled
- 10 cherry tomatoes, cut in half to 3 green onions
- 1/2 cup of cucumbers cups of lettuce
- 2 tablespoons of reduced-fat cheese Ranch Dressing or Catalina Dressing

Instructions:

- Place 3 oz of frozen chicken breast strips in the air fryer basket and cook the chicken breast for 12 minutes at 350.

- While the chicken is cooking slice the cucumbers and cherry tomatoes. To make the salad place 2 cups of lettuce, cucumbers, cherry tomatoes, hard-boiled eggs, (optional) cheese, and chopped chicken on top of the lettuce.

- The salad with Catalina or Ranch dressing on top. I typically don't count dressings for points and that is just what works for me.

Nutrient Value:

Calories: 536| Sugar: 6| Fat: 36| Saturated Fat: 6| Unsaturated Fat: 15|Carbohydrates: 28| Fiber: 13| Protein: 29

Egg Salad Poppers Recipe

Prep Time:

20mins

Ingredients:

- ¼ cup eggs, hard-boiled (chopped) 4 ounces Neufchatel cheese
- 2 Tablespoons Mayonnaise
- 2 Tablespoons spinach leaf (chopped) 2 Tablespoons green onion (minced) For the coating
- 2 Tablespoons THM Oat Fiber
- ¼ cup egg white
- 2 each Low Carb Whole Wheat Tortilla (toasted and crushed)

Instructions:

- In a medium bowl mix eggs, cheese, mayonnaise, spinach, and onion together.

- Scoop mixture into 1 TBS mounds on a parchment-lined sheet and freeze for 30 minutes.

- Preheat Air Fryer to 350° F

- Remove egg mounds from the freezer and roll in oat fiber, dip each one into the egg whites, and roll in the crushed low carb tortillas.

- Place coated egg salad balls onto your air fryer rack and bake for 6-8 minutes.

- Be careful when removing from your air fryer as these are delicate and the shell will break easily when they are hot.

- Allow cooling for a few minutes before eating. Can also be eaten cold when stored in the fridge.

Nutrient Value:

Calories: 239 Fat: 20g

Carbohydrates: 18g Sodium: 458mg Fiber: 14g

Protein: 11g Cholesterol: 79mg

Gluten Free Buffalo Cauliflower Salad

Prep Time:

Serves: 4 Salads 15 Mins Cook Time: 20 Min Total Time: 35 Min

Ingredients:

- 1/2 cup Frank's red hot sauce
- tablespoon coconut oil (or butter)
- Florets from 1 medium head of cauliflower 1/2 cup almond milk
- 1/2 cup water
- 3/4 cup almond flour
- teaspoons garlic powder 2 teaspoons onion powder 1 teaspoon paprika
- salt and pepper 2 celery ribs
- 1 cup halved cherry tomatoes (you can do this while you wait for the cauliflower to cook)
- ripe large avocado
- romaine hearts, chopped 1 cup shredded carrots
- to drizzle: ½ cup Ranch dressing

Instructions:

- Preheat an air fryer to 400 degrees.

- Place two large bowls next to each other on your workspace. In one bowl, whisk together the hot sauce and coconut oil. In the other bowl, whisk together almond milk, water, flour, garlic powder, onion powder, paprika, salt, and pepper. Add the cauliflower to the bowl. Dredge the cauliflower florets through the mixture and coat them well, patting the mixture into the crevices of the cauliflower. Using tongs (or your hands), transfer the dredged cauliflower into the hot sauce bowl and toss well to coat.

- Add the cauliflower in an even layer in the basket of the air fryer. Set for 10 minutes and halfway through, flip the cauliflower and let cook for an additional 5 minutes.

- While cauliflower cooks, prepare the rest of the recipe. Pour the hot sauce into a large bowl and set aside. Dice the celery, halve the cherry tomatoes, and peel, pit, and slice the avocado. Set everything aside.

- After you're done prepping the salad Ingredients, prepare the salads. Divide the romaine lettuce into bowls and drizzle each with 1 tablespoon of Ranch dressing. Divide the toppings onto the bowls (the celery, tomatoes, avocado, carrots) and once the cauliflower is done cooking, add that to the salad bowls. Drizzle with another tablespoon of Ranch dressing. Serve.

Nutrient Value:

Total Fat: 22g| Saturated Fat: 10g| Trans Fat: 0g| Unsaturated Fat: 12g| Cholesterol: 88mg| Sodium: 789mg| Carbohydrates: 2g| Fiber: 1g| Sugar: 0g| Protein: 29g

Air Fryer Coconut Shrimp Salad

Prep Time:

30 minutes Cook Time: 30 minutes Servings: 6 servings

Ingredients:

- Coconut Shrimp

- 2 lbs extra-large shrimp (13-15 per lb), peeled, tail-on 1 cup panko bread crumbs* (56 grams)

- 1/2 cup finely shredded sweetened coconut* (40 grams) 1/2 cup white whole wheat flour* (60 grams)

- 2 eggs

- 1/2 tsp each: salt and pepper

- Salad

- 10 cups baby spinach (325 grams)

- 2 medium mangos, peeled and chopped (650 grams) 2 small avocados, peeled and chopped (225 grams) 1 1/2 cups cherry tomatoes, halved (225 grams)

- 1/3 cup pickled red onion – recipe below (45 grams) 1/4 cup cilantro, chopped (5 grams)

- Sweet Chili Dressing

- 1/4 cup sweet Thai chili sauce (2 oz) 2 tbsp lime juice (1 oz)

- 2 tbsp coconut milk (1 oz)

Instructions:

- Whisk dressing ingredients until combined, set aside.

- Assemble the base of salad with spinach, mango, avocado, tomatoes, pickled red onion, and cilantro. Set aside in the refrigerator while prepping the shrimp.

- Add coconut and breadcrumbs to a bowl and mix until combined. Set aside.

- Add flour, salt, and pepper to a separate bowl and mix. Set aside. Add eggs to a third bowl and whisk. Set aside.

- Rinse and dry shrimp on a paper towel, then dip them one at a time into flour, then eggs, then breadcrumb mixture, coating the shrimp completely.

- Air fry shrimp at 380 degrees for 7-8 minutes or until breading is golden brown and shrimp is cooked through.

- Top salad base with shrimp and dressing and serve.

Nutrient Value:

Calories: 402

Calories From Fat: 108 Fat: 12g

Cholesterol: 289mg Sodium: 431mg Potassium: 797mg Carbohydrates: 37g
Fiber: 6g

Sugar: 22g Protein: 37g

Crispy Keto Air Fryer Pork Chops

Prep Time:

15 minutes Cook Time: 10 minutes Total Time: 25 minutes

Ingredients:

- Boneless Pork Chops
- 4–6 center-cut boneless pork chops (4–6 oz each, ~ ¾ inch thick) Keto Pork Chops Coating
- ⅓ cup almond flour
- ⅓ cup grated parmesan (or sub additional almond flour) 1 tsp garlic powder
- 1 tsp paprika
- ½ tsp onion powder
- ½ tsp salt
- ½ tsp black pepper 2 eggs

Instructions:

How To Air Fry Pork Chops

- Preheat air fryer to 400°F (200°C).

- Mix almond flour, grated parmesan, and seasonings in a shallow dish. In a separate dish, beat eggs.

- Coat pork chops in egg, and then coating mixture. Transfer coated chops to a plate.

- Spray both sides of coated chops with cooking spray, then add to the air fryer. Cook 3-4 at a time only. (Don't overcrowd your air fryer!)

- Cook boneless pork chops for 10 minutes, flipping halfway through. (Thicker chops and bone-in chops may need to cook for longer, 12-20 minutes.)

- After flipping, check the internal temperature of the pork every 1-2 minutes, until it reaches 145°F (63°C). To check the internal temperature, insert a meat thermometer straight into the side of the pork chop.

- Allow resting 3 minutes before slicing to reveal a perfect blush pink center.

- How To Oven Fry Pork Chops

- Preheat oven to 425°F (210°C).

- Prepare and coat keto pork chops as described above.

- Spray both sides of coated pork chops with cooking spray and add to a baking rack on top of a lined baking sheet.

- Bake for 20 minutes, flipping halfway through. (May need to bake longer for thicker chops or bone-in chops.)

- Near the end of cook time, check oven fried pork chops temperature as explained above.

Nutrient Value:

Calories:273| Sugar: 0.5g| Fat: 15g|Carbohydrates: 1g|Fiber: 0.5g|Protein: 30g

Air Fryer Buffalo Salmon Salad

Prep Time:

Total Time: 30 mins

Ingredients:

- 4 Tbsp. unsalted butter
- ¼ cup hot sauce
- 4 Verlasso salmon fillets (about 1 lb.) Cooking spray
- 1 large head romaine lettuce, chopped (about 8 cups)
- 1 ear of corn, kernels removed (or ½ cup frozen corn, thawed)
- ½ cup matchstick carrots
- 1 small red onion, thinly sliced 1 bell pepper, thinly sliced
- 3 stalks celery, chopped
- ¼ cup blue cheese crumbles
- Ranch or blue cheese dressing for serving, optional Additional hot sauce for serving, optional

Instructions:

- Melt butter in a small saucepan over medium heat. Remove pan from heat and stir in hot sauce.

- Place salmon in a baking pan and pour the sauce over salmon. Let marinate for 20-30 minutes, turning once halfway through.

- Preheat air fryer to 400°F. Lightly spray the fryer basket with cooking spray. Remove salmon from marinade and pat bottom (skin) dry. Place salmon in basket, skin side down, and cook for 7-10 minutes, or until salmon is cooked to desired doneness.

- While salmon is cooking, assemble the salad. Divide the lettuce among four bowls. Top each bowl with corn, carrots, onion, bell pepper, celery, and blue cheese. Place a salmon fillet on top of each salad.

- Drizzle with dressing and additional hot sauce if desired. Enjoy!

Nutrient Value:

Calories 360| Total Fat 22g|Cholesterol: 100mg| Sodium: 570mg| Total Carbohydrate: 14g| (Dietary: Fiber 5g| Total Sugars: 6g| Protein:28g

Grilled Romaine Salad

Prep Time:

15 mins Cook Time: 10 mins Servings: 4 servings

Ingredients:

- 2 medium heads of romaine lettuce, cut lengthwise into wedges Olive oil for brushing the romaine lettuce

- 1/2 cup crumbled or grated cheese (choose your favorite!) Lemon wedges for serving and squeezing over salad

- For The Dressing

- 2 cloves garlic, crushed or fine mince 3 tablespoons olive oil for the dressing Zest of 1 fresh lemon

- 2 tablespoons fresh lemon juice 1 tablespoon balsamic vinegar 1/2 teaspoon dijon mustard

- teaspoon soy sauce (use tamari for gluten free) 1 teaspoon brown sugar

- 1/2 teaspoon paprika

- 1/2 teaspoon kosher salt, or to taste Black pepper to taste

Instructions:

Make The Dressing

- Whisk together the dressing ingredients (garlic, olive oil, lemon zest, lemon juice, balsamic, mustard, soy sauce, brown sugar, paprika, salt, and black pepper). Set aside.

- Heat the grill to medium-high to high heat (depending on the grill's heat intensity). Make sure to scrape the grill grates so they are clean & food won't stick as easily.

- Lightly coat the romaine lettuce heads with oil. Grill the romaine until they're gently cooked and slightly charred.

- Allow grilled romaine to cool. Lay on a serving tray, drizzle dressing on top, and sprinkle with cheese. Serve with lemon wedges and enjoy!

Nutrient Value:

Calories: 165kcal | Carbohydrates: 4g | Protein: 4g | Fat: 15g | Saturated Fat: 4g | Cholesterol: 15mg | Sodium: 472mg | Potassium: 48mg | Fiber: 1g | Sugar: 2g | Vitamin C: 4mg | Calcium: 109mg | Iron: 0.3mg

Air Fryer Sesame Ginger Salmon With Spicy Cucumber Salad

Prep Time:

10mins Cook time: 8mins

Ingredients:

- 1/ 3 cup Annie's Organic Sesame Ginger Vinaigrette 1 pound salmon, cut into 4 portions
- hothouse cucumbers, thinly sliced 1 jalapeño, thinly sliced
- A handful of fresh mint leaves, chopped 1/ 2 cup seasoned rice vinegar
- 1/ 2 teaspoon salt 1 teaspoon sugar
- Method
- Pour ¼ cup Annie's Sesame Ginger Vinaigrette into the bottom of a medium bowl or baking dish
- Marinate salmon portions skin side facing up in dish for 5 minutes
- Mix cucumber slices, hot pepper, mint, vinegar, salt, + sugar in a large mason jar or medium bowl. Chill cucumber salad in the refrigerator, stirring every 5 minutes while salmon is cooking.
- After salmon has marinated for 5 minutes, place skin side down in air fryer
- Air Fry at 400°F for 8 minutes
- Drizzle salmon with remaining vinaigrette and air fry an additional 1-2 minutes until cooked through, browned, and crispy on the edges
- Using a slotted spoon to eliminate excess pickling juices, place ¼ cucumber salad topped with 1 salmon portion on each plate. Serve immediately!

Nutrient Value:

Calories: 122| Fat: 8g| Sat fat: 2g| Unsatfat: 5g| Protein: 10g| Carbohydrate| 0g Fiber 0g| Sugars 0g| Added sugars: 0g| Sodium: 254mg

Citrus & Avocado Salad

Prep Time:

10 Mins Total Time: 10 minutes

Ingredients:

- 1/2 red grapefruit 1 blood orange
- 1 Navel orange 1/2 avocado
- 1/4 cup chopped roasted pistachios 2 Tbsp. chives
- Tbsp. blood orange infused olive oil Sea salt & black pepper to taste!

Instructions:

- Slice all citrus in whole circular thin slices.

- Arrange citrus on a large plate and top with avocado slices.

- Garnish with chopped chives, pistachios, blood orange olive oil, sea salt, and pepper.

Nutrient Value:

Total Fat: 22g| Saturated Fat: 10g| Trans Fat: 0g| Unsaturated Fat: 12g| Cholesterol: 88mg| Sodium: 789mg| Carbohydrates: 2g| Fiber: 1g| Sugar: 0g| Protein: 29g

Air Fryer Croutons

Prep Time:

Total Time: 30 mins

Ingredients:

- 4 slices bread
- 2 tablespoons melted butter 1 teaspoon parsley
- 1/2 teaspoon onion powder 1/2 teaspoon seasoned salt 1/2 teaspoon garlic salt

Instructions:

- Preheat the air fryer to 390 degrees.

- Cut 4 slices of bread into bite-sized pieces.

- Melt butter, and place butter into a medium-sized bowl.

- Add 1 teaspoon parsley, 1/2 teaspoon seasoned salt, 1/2 teaspoon garlic salt, 1/2 teaspoon of onion powder to the melted butter. Stir well.

- Add bread to the bowl and carefully stir to coat the bread so that it is coated by the seasoned butter.

- Place buttered bread into the air fryer basket.

- Cook for 5 to 7 minutes or until the bread is toasted. Serve immediately.

Nutrient Value:

Calories: 127kcal | Carbohydrates: 14g | Protein: 3g | Fat: 7g | Saturated Fat: 4g | Cholesterol: 15mg | Sodium: 777mg | Potassium: 51mg | Fiber: 1g | Sugar: 2g | Vitamin A: 175IU | Calcium: 39mg | Iron: 1mg

Instant Pot Southern-Style Potato Salad

Prep Time:

15 minutes Cook Time: 4 minutes Chill Time: 1 hour

Total Time1 hour 19 minutes

Ingredients:

- 1 1/2 cups water

- 5 (about 2 pounds total) russet potatoes peeled and sliced into 1 1/2 inch cubes

- 4 eggs

- 1 large bowl of cold water ice added to the water is optional 1 cup mayo

- 1/2 cup white onions chopped 1/4 cup pickle relish

- tablespoon yellow mustard salt and pepper to taste

- Lawry's seasoning salt to taste optional 1 teaspoon paprika

Instructions:

- Add the water to the Instant Pot. Place the Instant Pot on the saute' function. This will allow the water to warm so that it comes to pressure sooner.

- While the water heats up slice the potatoes.

- Add the steamer basket to the pot. Place the potatoes on top of the basket. Season the potatoes with about 1/4 teaspoon of salt.

- Place the eggs on the very top of the potatoes.

- Close the pot and seal. Cook for 4 minutes on Manual > High-Pressure Cooking.

- When the Instant Pot indicates it has finished cooking, quick release the steam.

- Remove the eggs and place them in the bowl of cold water for 5 minutes.

- Remove the potatoes and transfer to a large bowl. Peel the eggs and slice them into small cubes.

- Add the cooked eggs, mayo, mustard, relish, white onions, paprika, and salt and pepper to taste to the mixture. Taste repeatedly. You may need to add additional salt and pepper.

- (If you prefer sweet potato salad add a little more relish and maybe sugar.)

- Stir to combine.

- Cover and chill for at least an hour to two hours before serving.

Nutrient Value:

Calories: 247kcal | Carbohydrates: 13g | Protein: 4g | Fat: 20g

Grilled Romaine Salad

Prep Time:

10 Minutes Cook Time: 2 Minutes Total Time: 12 Minutes

Ingredients:

- heads of romaine lettuce 6 slices of bacon
- 6 oz. pomegranate seeds
- 6 oz. of blue cheese crumbles
- 12 oz. of blue cheese dressing (see recipe card below) 4 tbsp of olive oil
- 1 tbsp balsamic glaze

Instructions:

- Cook the bacon in an air fryer at 370°F for 8-12 minutes until crispy and slice into crumbles. Check out the recipe for the best air fryer bacon.

- Slice the heads of romaine in half, lengthwise. Brush the romaine lettuce with olive oil.

- Place the romaine cut side down on the medium-hot grill.

- Flip the heads of romaine after 1-2 minutes and cook on for equal time on the other side.

- Transfer the romaine cut side up to a serving platter and pile on the bacon, pomegranate seeds, and blue cheese crumbles.

- Finish by drizzling the amazing blue cheese salad dressing over the grilled romaine (see recipe below)

- Drizzle with a sweet balsamic glaze, and serve.

Nutrient Value:

Total Fat: 51g Saturated Fat: 13g Trans Fat: 1g Unsaturated Fat: 36g Cholesterol: 50mg Sodium: 901mg Carbohydrates: 17g Fiber: 6g

Sugar: 10g Protein: 14g

Roasted Sumac Cauliflower Mediterranean Salad

Prep Time:

20 mins Cook Time: 5 mins

Ingredients:

- 4 tbsp Hummus
- 1 cup cooked chickpeas
- Roasted Cauliflower
- 1 small head cauliflower
- tsp Cured Sumac I used Burlap & Barrel 1 tsp garlic powder
- tbsp extra virgin olive oil
- Mediterranean Tomato-Cucumber-Mint Salad
- 2 Persian cucumbers chopped into 1/2 inch pieces 1/4 cup red onion diced
- cup cherry tomatoes or mini San Marzano Tomatoes sliced in half 2 sprigs mint Julienned
- tsp lemon juice
- 1 tbsp extra virgin olive oil

Instructions:

- Prepare the Hummus

- Roast The Cauliflower

- In a mixing bowl, coat the florets in a few drizzles of olive oil and about 1 tsp cured sumac and 1 tsp garlic powder. Add salt and pepper to taste. Mix well to combine.

- Set Air Fryer to 400° and air fry the cauliflower for 7 minutes.

- Remove the basket and shake and air fry for an additional 7 minutes until the edges are brown and crispy.

- If you don't have an air fryer, lay florets on a baking tray and roast at 425° for 20-25 minutes

- Prepare The Tomato-Cucumber-Mint Salad

- Assemble all ingredients in a small bowl and mix well. Assemble the Bowl

- Layer some salad greens into a large bowl.

- Add a handful of cauliflower, some tomato-cucumber-mint salad, a few tablespoons of hummus, and a handful of chickpeas.

- Serve with lemon wedges or with some balsamic vinegar and olive oil and some toasted pita bread.

Salade Niçoise | Air Fryer Recipe

Prep Time:

15 minutes Cook Time: 20 minutes Total Time: 35 minutes

Ingredients:

- 6 Baby New Potatoes, quartered
- 2 teaspoons Vegetable Oil, plus additional for tuna salt and ground black pepper
- 1 cup slender green beans, trimmed and snapped in half 2 4 ounce tuna fillets, about 1 inch thick, cut in half
- cup Cherry Tomatoes, halved 6 butter lettuce leaves
- hard-boiled eggs, peeled and halved 10 Nicoise olives
- For The Vinaigrette
- 2 tablespoons Olive Oil
- 1 tablespoon Red Wine Vinegar 1/8 teaspoon, salt
- 1 teaspoon Dijon mustard
- 1/4 teaspoon Herbes de Provence, (optional) Ground Black Pepper

Instructions:

- **For The Salad:** In a small bowl, toss potatoes, green beans, and grape tomatoes with 2 teaspoons of vegetable oil, salt, and pepper. Arrange the vegetables in a single layer in an air fryer basket. Set fryer to 400°F for 10 minutes, shaking halfway through cook time.

- After 10 minutes of cook time, brush tuna on both sides with 1 tablespoon vegetable oil and season to taste with salt and coarsely ground pepper. Press the salt and pepper into the tuna so they will stay put. Add tuna to the basket on top of the vegetables. Cook for 5 minutes for tuna that is cooked medium-well.

- At end of cook time, remove the tuna and let it rest for 5 minutes. Slice tuna thinly across the grain.

- Meanwhile, for the vinaigrette: Combine vinegar, salt, mustard, olive oil, black pepper, and Herbes de Provence to taste in a small jar with a lid. Shake to combine.

- Place 3 lettuce leaves on each of two dinner plates. Arrange tuna, green beans, tomatoes, and potatoes in small piles on lettuce. Place 2 egg halves on each plate. Scatter olives over. Drizzle all with the vinaigrette. Serve immediately.

Nutrient Value:

Calories: 601kcal | Carbohydrates: 49g | Protein: 41g | Fat: 27g | Fiber: 8g | Sugar: 7g

Air Fryer Kale

Prep Time:

5 mins Cook Time: 3 mins

Ingredients:

- 3.5 ounces kale leaves 100 grams or 2-3 cups Oil spray
- Salt to taste optional

Instructions:

- Preheat air fryer to 350 degrees F (175 C) for at least 5 minutes

- While the air fryer preheats, wash and dry the kale leaves thoroughly. Remove the stems from the leaves if desired (see note). Slice the leaves into very thin strips.

- When the air fryer has finished preheating, add the sliced kale into the basket. Spray the leaves with oil as you shake the basket. Season lightly with salt (if using). Make sure the leaves are spread evenly across the basket before you put the basket back in the fryer.

- Air fry for 3 minutes, pausing briefly after 1.5 or 2 minutes to shake and agitate the kale. Serve immediately.

Nutrient Value:

Total Fat: 22g| Saturated Fat: 10g| Trans Fat: 0g| Unsaturated Fat: 12g| Cholesterol: 88mg| Sodium: 789mg| Carbohydrates: 2g| Fiber: 1g| Sugar: 0g| Protein: 29g

Chopped Salad With Japanese Sweet Potato Croutons

Prep Time:

Total Time: 30 mins

Ingredients:

- pound salad mixture including greens and vegetables of your choice 1 each crisp sweet apple, cored and diced

- each mandarin oranges, peeled, segmented & cut in half 1/3 cup pomegranate seeds

- 8-12 ounce baked Japanese Sweet Potato cold, cut into pieces with skin on tbsp Sweet Balsamic Vinegar 4% acidity Nappa Valley Naturals Grand Reserve or California Balsamic Simply Lemon are two of my favorites for this salad.

Instructions:

- To make the JSP croutons, place the cold diced sweet potato pieces in a cold air fryer set to 400 degrees. Air fry for about 20 minutes or until golden brown. If You don't have an air fryer you can crisp them up under the broiler. Watch them carefully as they go from lightly brown to burnt in a hurry.

- While the croutons are in the air fryer, chop the salad with a mezzaluna knife in a wood bowl or you can use a large knife and a large cutting board or one of the other methods I show in my video on how to chop a salad without a wood bowl.\

- Add the diced apple, mandarin oranges, pomegranate seeds, JSP croutons, and the balsamic vinegar of your choice. Gently stir all of the **Ingredients:** together and place it in a pretty bowl to serve. Many different flavors would work well with this salad. Don't add the vinegar until you are ready to serve the salad as it is best served freshly tossed.

Nutrient Value:

Total fat: 30.8gg Sodium: 1321.9mg Sugar: 6.7g

Vitamin A: 567.5ug

Carbohydrates: 21.4g Protein:29.8g Vitamin C: 56.8mg

Crisp Pork Belly With Coriander Salad

Prep Time:

1 day

Cook Time: 40 minutes

Ingredients:

- Pork Belly
- 1 kg pork belly Salt
- Coriander Salad Ingredients
- 1 cup washed coriander leaves including stems roughly chopped
- ½ medium red onion very finely sliced
- medium red chili finely chopped or to taste
- ¼ cup toasted white sesame seeds
- ⅓ cup roasted chopped unsalted peanuts
- Coriander Salad Dressing Ingredients
- tablespoons sesame oil or EVOO- extra virgin olive oil
- 2 tablespoons rice wine vinegar or apple cider vinegar (ACV)/white vinegar
- ½ tablespoon tamari or soy sauce
- teaspoon stevia blend or sweetener of choice

Instructions:

- Prepare the pork belly by washing and drying with a paper towel. Rub with salt and leave it in the fridge overnight to dry out covered with paper toweling or a cloth.

- Just before cooking removes the pork from the fridge and score the fat horizontally and vertically about 1 cm/.4 " or visually score it so that the score lines will coincide with the cutting line when you slice the pork belly to serve. Rub some additional salt into the pork rind.

- Air Fryer Pork Belly Method

- Preheat the air fryer to 200 C/390 F.

- Cook the pork belly rind side down for 10 minutes. This helps prevent the pork belly from curling up.

- Turn the heat down to 180 C/ 360 F and turn the pork belly over so the rind side is on top. Continue to cook for a further 30 minutes or until the pork belly is cooked and tender. Allow the pork to rest for about 20 minutes before slicing into approximately 2cm/.8" slices or as you prefer.

- Conventional Oven Pork Belly Method

- Preheat the oven to 200 C/ 290 F.

- Place the pork rind side in a baking dish. Cook the pork for 20-25 minutes. If your oven is baking unevenly, turn your pork belly around and bake for a further 20-25 minutes or until the pork belly is cooked and tender. Allow the pork to rest for about 20 minutes before slicing into approximately 2cm/.8" slices or as you prefer.

- Coriander Salad

Instructions:

- Combine the dressing ingredients and mix them so the sweetener dissolves.

- Mix all of the salad Ingredients in a medium bowl.

- Mix the dressing through the salad and serve on the side of the pork belly.

Nutrient Value:

Calories: 476kcal | Carbohydrates: 4g | Protein: 54g | Fat: 25g | Fiber: 2g

Air Fried Chicken Cordon Bleu Salad

Prep Time:

10 Minutes Cook Time: 12 Minutes Total Time: 22 Minutes

Ingredients:

- boneless, skinless chicken breasts 2 tablespoons flour
- 1 egg, beaten
- 1/4 cup seasoned bread crumbs
- 4 tablespoons white wine vinegar
- 2 tablespoons nonfat plain Greek yogurt 2 Tablespoons Dijon mustard
- 2 Tablespoons honey 4 tablespoons olive oil 8 slices deli ham
- 4 slices Swiss cheese, cut in half 12 cups lettuce
- 1 seedless cucumber, chopped 1 cup tomatoes, halved
- 1/4 cup thinly sliced red onion

Instructions:

- Lightly coat the chicken with flour, then dip it into the egg. Dredge in bread crumbs to coat. Spritz with oil.

- Air fry at 400 degrees for 12 minutes, or until cooked through. Slice into bite-sized pieces.

- Meanwhile, make the dressing by whisking together the vinegar, yogurt, mustard, and honey until smooth. Drizzle in the olive oil. Season with salt and pepper.

- Layer together one piece of ham and one piece of cheese. Roll together, then slice into 4 pinwheels. Repeat with remaining ham and cheese.

- Pile the lettuce onto a platter. Top with cucumber, tomatoes, onion, chicken, and ham and cheese pinwheels. Drizzle with dressing.

Nutrient Value:

Total Fat: 28g Saturated Fat: 8g

Trans Fat: 0g Unsaturated Fat: 17g Cholesterol: 139mg Sodium: 909mg Carbohydrates: 27g Fiber: 5g Sugar: 13g Protein: 39g

Alphabetical Index

V

CPSIA information can be obtained
at www.ICGtesting.com
Printed in the USA
LVHW081202270521
688664LV00006B/671